Kids' Backyard Safari

RED FOXES

CURIOUS FOX BOOKS

CURIOUS FOX BOOKS

ISBN 979-8-89094-000-1

Library of Congress Control Number: 2023942299

ABOUT THE AUTHOR: Nicole Orr has been writing for ten years. In that time, she's participated in National Novel Writing Month eight times, written over 30 fictional novels for fun, and become a freelance transcriptionist. Since finishing this book, Orr has been eager to write zombie foxes into her next novel.

To learn more about the other great books from Fox Chapel Publishing, or to find a retailer near you, call toll-free 800-457-9112 or visit us at *www.FoxChapelPublishing.com*.

We are always looking for talented authors. To submit an idea, please send a brief inquiry to acquisitions@foxchapelpublishing.com.

Fox Chapel Publishing makes every effort to use environmentally friendly paper for printing.

Printed in China
First Printing

Kids' Backyard Safari

RED FOXES

Explore Their World and Learn Fun Facts

Nicole Orr

Imagine it is a cold winter night in the woods and you are camping in a cabin. You hear a wailing noise and look out the window. Is it a ghost? No! It is the cry of a red fox and you're about to go on a backyard safari to meet them!

Red foxes are even hairier than they look! Not only do they have whiskers on their face, but they have them on their legs, too.

Look at a fox's eyes. Do they look more like a dog's or a cat's? If you guessed a cat's, you're right! Just like cats, foxes can see in the dark, too.

A group of foxes is called a skulk. Don't confuse it with a skunk. Skunks are smellier!

When you walk outside the next morning, you see that the ground is covered in fox prints. The sound from the night before was made by a female fox, known as a vixen. She was probably searching for a mate. The males, called dogs, fight over vixens. The strongest dog wins.

What do human kids have in common with fox pups? They both like to wrestle and jump high up in the air!

Adult foxes make at least 12 sounds and pups make at least 8. Fox sounds mean different things, like saying hello, showing anger, or sending warnings. They can yelp, bark, wail, and "gekker," which is a type of throaty chattering. Foxes gekker when they're nervous or play-fighting. Do you think you can gekker?

They might look scary, but foxes are very friendly compared to other wild animals. They will attack if they feel threatened, but they are usually peaceful and avoid conflict with people and their pets.

Foxes usually have four to six babies at a time. The pups have fine gray hair and are very small—they could fit in your hand! They are born blind, and their eyes start to open when they're around nine days old. When they're a month old, they leave their den and wrestle and play with each other. At 12 weeks old, their parents start to show them how to hunt and forage.

In many fairy tales, foxes are sneaky and very clever.

A dog teaches his pups how to hunt. They all sit quietly next to a burrow until a mouse sticks its head out. They sneak up, running and pouncing to surprise their prey.

Pups find it fun to chew on each other's ears and tails.

Male foxes aren't just called dogs. Sometimes they're called reynards. *Renard* is the French word for fox!

The mice and other small animals foxes hunt don't see them because their red fur blends in with leaves and bushes. Foxes are very fast, too. They can run 31 miles per hour (50 kilometers per hour)—half as fast as a car on the highway.

Foxes have excellent hearing, too. They hear animals like rabbits burrowing underground even beneath the snow. Then they dig down or pounce on their targets.

Rabbits are one of the fox's favorite foods. If there are a lot of rabbits in a part of the woods, chances are there will be a lot of foxes there, too.

Foxes are born with blue eyes. As adults, their eyes turn brown.

The whiskers of foxes are very sensitive. They can even feel prey moving through the grass.

Foxes also snack on birds, bugs, berries, and even worms. If the dog brings back more food than his family can eat, he buries it for later. This is called caching. Foxes also pee on their territory to signal to other animals that it is protected. This is called scent marking.

Many human kids don't like to eat their veggies. Some foxes don't either! They eat mostly meats and fruits.

Red foxes live in dens, called earths. Sometimes they make them out of leftover holes from other animals, and sometimes they dig their own. They use their tail, known as a brush, like a blanket to keep themselves and any babies warm.

Most fox dens are made to face the sun. Why? Because this helps keep the pups warm.

Some foxes, known as urban foxes, live in cities. Many people think of them as nuisances since they eat out of trash cans, steal pet food, and make messes. In the wild, foxes live only five or six years. In the city, there are more dangers. There are big cars. There are big dogs. There are big humans. These are all threats.

What does a fox's fur smell like? A little like a skunk. Foxes have two scent glands. These make a smell that scares off enemies.

A vixen uses her tongue to get tough seeds out of her tail.

Foxes are a lot like cats. They like to eat mice, and they use their tongues to stay clean. But foxes are not related to cats. They are part of the dog family.

The next time you are camping and hear a ghostly wail in the middle of the night, don't be afraid. Now you know it's just the cry of a red fox.

What is one of the best ways to know what foxes eat? Look at their poo, also called scat.

FURTHER READING

Fiction Books Featuring Foxes

Geisel, Theodor. *Fox in Socks: Dr. Seuss's Book of Tongue Tanglers.* Random House Books for Young Readers: New York, 2011.

Gliori, Debi. *No Matter What.* Houghton Mifflin Harcourt Books for Young Readers: Boston, 2008.

Gliori, Debi. *Stormy Weather.* Walker Children's: London, 2009.

Spinelli, Eileen. *Miss Fox's Class Shapes Up.* Albert Whitman and Company: Morton Grove, IL, 2011.

Spinelli, Eileen. *Peace Week in Miss Fox's Class.* Albert Whitman and Company: Morton Grove, IL, 2009.

Works Consulted

Lantier, Patricia, and Judy Schuler. *The Wonder of Foxes.* Gareth Stevens Publishing: Milwaukee, 2001.

Leach, Michael. *Fox.* PowerKIDS Press: New York, 2009.

Lockwood, Sophie. *Foxes.* The Child's World: Mankato, MN, 2008.

McDonald, Mary Ann. *Foxes.* The Child's World: Mankato, MN, 2008.

Person, Stephen. *Arctic Fox.* Bearport Publishing, Inc.: New York, 2009.

Phillips, Dee. *Fox's Den.* Bearport Publishing, Inc.: New York, 2012.

"Red Foxes," *National Geographic A–Z.* Accessed: September 12, 2013. https://www.nationalgeographic.com/animals/mammals/facts/red-fox?source=A-to-Z

On the Internet

Animals Time: Red Fox Facts for Kids, http://animalstime.com/red-fox-facts-kids-red-fox-habitat-diet/

Environmental Education for Kids (EEK): Red Fox, https://www.eekwi.org/animals/mammals/red-fox

Switch Zoo: Red Fox, https://switchzoo.com/profiles/redfox.htm

INDEX

PHOTO CREDITS: pp. 4-5—Chris Parker; pp. 6-7—Rob, pp.14-15—Peter Trimming, pp. 18-19—Jim the Photographer; p 22-23—Likaduck; pp. 26-27—Olly Scott; 28-29—Tambako the Jaguar; pp. 30-31—Peter Trimming; all other photos—Public Domain. Every measure has been taken to find all copyright holders of material used in this book. In the event any mistakes or omissions have happened within, attempts to correct them will be made in future editions of the book.